Midge and Gran run away

Midge's mum and dad
are on holiday.
"They never take me,"
Midge says to Gran.

Gran nudges Midge gently.
"Let's have some fun,"
she urges.

Midge thinks.

"Let's run away!" he says.

"Run away?" Gran says.

"Fantastic!"

Midge puts ginger fudge in his backpack. Gran puts fudge in her backpack, too.

Off they run, down the street
and over bridge number one.
They run along the track and
over bridge number two.

Then they run over
bridge number three.

"Where are we going?"
Gran puffs.
"To the beach," says Midge.

They run to the edge of
the water. They dodge the
waves. They look for shells.

"Stop!" says Gran.
"I need some ginger fudge."
So they sit near a hedge and
eat some fudge.

"Now let's get frozen yogurts," Midge says. "May I have two large mango and coconut tubs?" he asks.

They eat from the giant
tubs as they walk along
a ridge to the park.

They swing on the swing
and Midge slides on the slide.
Gran slides on the slide, too.

"I'm tired," Midge says.
"Let's run home."
They run home over the
three bridges.

They eat the remaining
bit of fudge for tea.
"That was the best day
ever," Midge says.
He and Gran fall asleep.

Words to blend

urges	large	Midge
nudges	fudge	bridge
edge	dodge	ridge
gently	ginger	giant
hedge	never	fantastic
coconut	shells	tubs

Midge and Gran run away   Level 7, Set 2a, Story 93

Before reading

Synopsis: Midge and Gran decide to have some fun by running away to the beach.

Review phonemes and graphemes: /ear/ ere, eer; /air/ are, ear, ere

Focus phoneme: /j/ **Focus graphemes:** ge, dge, g

Story discussion: Look at the cover, and read the title together. Ask: *Who do you think Midge and Gran are? What kind of book do you think this is, fiction or non-fiction? How do you know? What do you think might happen in this book?*

Link to prior learning: Remind children that the sound /j/ as in 'jam' can also be spelled 'ge', 'dge' and 'g'. Turn to page 3 and ask children to find words with the /j/ sound (nudges, Midge, urges, gently).

Vocabulary check: nudge: gently poke with your elbow – 'Gran nudges Midge' means 'Gran gently pokes Midge with her elbow'.

Decoding practice: Display the words 'giant', 'hedge', 'large' and 'bridge'. Can children circle the letter string that makes the /j/ sound, and read each word?

Tricky word practice: Display the word 'two'. Tell children that the tricky bit of this word is 'wo', which says /oo/ as in moon. Practise reading and spelling this word.

After reading

Apply learning: Discuss the book. Ask: *Do you think Midge and Gran's day looked like fun? Would you do anything differently? If yes, what would you change?*

Comprehension

- How many bridges did Midge and Gran cross? (three)
- Did Midge and Gran eat ginger fudge before or after getting to the beach? (after)
- Which did Midge and Gran eat first, fudge or frozen yogurt? (fudge)

Fluency

- Pick a page that most of the group read quite easily. Ask them to reread it with pace and expression. Model how to do this if necessary.
- Children can read Midge's words on page 12. Challenge children to read the second bit of speech as if they were really asking for yogurt tubs.
- Practise reading the words on page 17.

Tricky words review

are	says	ask
have	some	once
two	the	of
was	one	water
school	laugh	thought